DATE DUE

NOV 1 5 2010			
DEC 1 5			
NDEC 1 8			
APR 0 3			
MAY 1 3			

Demco

SPORTS INJURIES:
HOW TO PREVENT, DIAGNOSE, & TREAT

FIELD

Sports Injuries:
How to Prevent, Diagnose, & Treat

- Baseball
- Basketball
- Cheerleading
- Equestrian
- Extreme Sports
- Field
- Field Hockey
- Football
- Gymnastics
- Hockey
- Ice Skating
- Lacrosse
- Soccer
- Track
- Volleyball
- Weight Training
- Wrestling

SPORTS INJURIES:
HOW TO PREVENT, DIAGNOSE, & TREAT

FIELD

CHRIS McNAB

MASON CREST PUBLISHERS
www.masoncrest.com

Mason Crest Publishers Inc.
370 Reed Road
Broomall, PA 19008
(866) MCP-BOOK (toll free)
www.masoncrest.com

First printing

1 2 3 4 5 6 7 8 9 10

Library of Congress Cataloging-in-Publication Data on file
at the Library of Congress

ISBN 1-59084-639-7

Series ISBN 1-59084-625-7

Editorial and design by
Amber Books Ltd.
Bradley's Close
74–77 White Lion Street
London N1 9PF
www.amberbooks.co.uk

Project Editor: Michael Spilling
Design: Graham Curd
Picture Research: Natasha Jones

Printed and bound in the Hashemite Kingdom of Jordan

PICTURE CREDITS
Corbis: 6, 13, 16, 20, 22, 23, 24, 29, 30, 33, 35, 38, 40, 42, 48, 51, 52, 54-55, 57;
©EMPICS: 15, 18, 36, 59; **Mary Evans Picture Library**: 8, 10, 11, 14.

FRONT COVER: All ©EMPICS except Corbis (bl).

ILLUSTRATIONS: Courtesy of Amber Books except:
Bright Star Publishing plc: 45, 46, 49.

IMPORTANT NOTICE

This book is intended to provide general information about sports injuries, their prevention, and their treatment.
The information contained herein is not intended as a substitute for professional medical care. Always consult a
doctor before beginning any exercise program, and for diagnosis and treatment of any injury. Accordingly, the
publisher cannot accept any responsibility for any prosecution or proceedings brought or instituted against any
person or body as a result of the use or misuse of the techniques and information within.

CONTENTS

Foreword   6

Field Events   8

Mental Preparation to Avoid Injury   16

Physical Preparation   24

Using Equipment Safely   34

Treating Common Injuries   40

Careers in Field Athletics   52

Glossary   60

Further Information   62

Index   64

Foreword

Sports Injuries: How to Prevent, Diagnose, and Treat is a seventeen-volume series written for young people who are interested in learning about various sports and how to participate in them safely. Each volume examines the history of the sport and the rules of play; it also acts as a guide for prevention and treatment of injuries, and includes instruction on stretching, warming up, and strength training, all of which can help players avoid the most common musculoskeletal injuries. *Sports Injuries* offers ways for readers to improve their performance and gain more enjoyment from playing sports, and young athletes will find these volumes informative and helpful in their pursuit of excellence.

Sports medicine professionals assigned to a sport that they are not familiar with can also benefit from this series. For example, a football athletic trainer may need to provide medical care for a local gymnastics meet. Although the emergency medical principles and action plan would remain the same, the athletic trainer could provide better care for the gymnasts after reading a simple overview of the principles of gymnastics in *Sports Injuries*.

Although these books offer an overview, they are not intended to be comprehensive in the recognition and management of sports injuries. The text helps the reader appreciate and gain awareness of the common injuries possible during participation in sports. Reference material and directed readings are provided for those who want to delve further into the subject.

Written in a direct and easily accessible style, *Sports Injuries* is an enjoyable series that will help young people learn about sports and sports medicine.

Susan Saliba, Ph.D., National Athletic Trainers' Association Education Council

American track and field athlete Carl Lewis qualifies for the long jump at the Pan American Games in 1987.

Field Events

Within athletics, field events are some of the most ancient sports. Events such as the javelin and shot date back to prehistorical times, the shot being thrown in aggression and the javelin being used in warfare. Both are now tests of supreme athletic ability.

Most field events originated in activities other than sports. Discus throwing, for example, probably came from the ancient practice of soldiers throwing their shields across rivers before fording a crossing. The javelin and shot put also had military origins: javelins were used in combat by around the third millennium B.C.E., and the origins of the shot put date back to prehistory, when heavy rocks were hurled in aggression against animals or other humans. Slowly these instruments of war became instruments of sport.

Some field events, however, were created as sports. The Celts—a people who spread throughout Europe in the first and second millennia B.C.E.—were great sporting innovators. The long jump was a part of Celtic games as far back as 2000 B.C.E. and was included in the ancient Olympics. Celtic peoples also introduced a version of the high jump.

Over the centuries, existing field events were refined and new ones created. In the fourteenth century C.E., shot putters received a new object to throw—iron cannon balls, which are very like the modern shot put. From the same century emerged

Discus throwers of ancient Greece compete. Note the difference in throwing technique from today's discus competitors. Many of today's techniques in throwing events were only developed in the twentieth century.

hammer throwing, and the hammer was at that time literally just that, a blacksmith's iron hammer. As for the pole vault, this emerged from a medieval method of crossing ditches and rivers.

Until the ninteenth century, field events were a scattered group of sports, with varying rules and equally varied equipment. It was in nineteenth-century England that field events were standardized, mostly in the public schools and colleges, with their emphasis on sporting achievement and experimentation. With the revival of the Olympics in 1896, field events took their place alongside running events, and together they became track and field. By the end of the nineteenth century, almost all the events we know

A javelin thrower in the 1932 Olympics, who threw the javelin 238.55 feet (72.71 m). Today's javelin throwers easily achieve distances of around 330 feet (100 m), such are improvements in training and technique.

today had been established. One important point is that field events were still dominated by men. It would be well into the twentieth century before women were able to compete in these events. Whereas the discus was thrown by men at the 1896 Olympics in Greece, women would not compete in the same event until the 1928 Olympics in Amsterdam. In the hammer throw, there was a full century between the first men's Olympic competition in Paris in 1900 and the women's first Olympic competition in Sydney in 2000.

MODERN FIELD EVENTS

There are currently eight basic field events: javelin, hammer throw, discus, shot put, pole vault, long jump, triple jump, and high jump. Here we will look at these events as they appear in Olympic competition.

Javelin

The javelin event is a simple test of who can throw the farthest, although the javelin must touch the floor point-first to qualify as a legal throw. For men, the javelin is 8 ft 6 in–8 ft 10 in (2.6–2.7 m) long and weighs 1 lb 12 oz (800 g). In the women's event, the javelin is 7 ft 2 in–7 ft 6 in (2.2–2.3 m) long and weighs 1 lb 5 oz (600 g). The javelin is thrown over a course about 330 ft (100 m) long. Judges use long tapes to measure the throw distance from the edge of the **stopboard** to the landing point. Depending on the number of competitors in the event, the athlete will throw either three or six times.

Pat O'Callaghan of Ireland prepares to hurl the hammer at the 1932 Olympics. Very few field athletes in this era were professional.

Discus

The discus is a challenging technical event, requiring timing, balance, and accuracy. Two sizes and weights of discus are used, according to whether men or women are competing. The men's discus weighs 4 pounds 6 ounces (2 kg), measures about $8^3/_4$ inches (219–221mm) in diameter, and is 2 inches (46 mm) thick. The women's equivalent is half the weight, about 7 inches (180–182 mm) wide, and about $1^1/_2$ inches (37–39 mm) thick.

Throwing the discus is done from a circular area 8 feet 2 inches (2.5 m) in diameter, three-quarters of which is surrounded by a protective cage. The discus is thrown out into a fan-shaped area that opens to an angle of 40°. The judges measure the distance thrown from the edge of the throwing circle to the point of landing

Hammer throw

The hammer throw is done from the same throwing area and protective cage as the discus. The protective cage is even more essential, as the head of the men's hammer is a potentially lethal ball of metal weighing 16 pounds (7.25 kg), swung on the end of a chain 4 foot (1.215 m) long. The women's hammer is 8 pounds 13 ounces (4 kg), and the chain is 3 feet 11 inches (1.2 m) long. To throw, the athlete grips the handle at the end of the chain and makes a complex rotational movement before releasing the hammer down the field.

The men's hammer-throw record currently stands at 285 feet (86.86 m) by Yuriy Sedykh of the Soviet Union in 1986, and the women's at 249 feet (75.89 m) by Mihaela Melinte of Romania in 1999.

Shot put

A shot put is a ball of heavy metal weighing 16 pounds (7.25 kg) in the men's competition and 8 pounds 13 ounces (4 kg) in the women's events. The athlete launches the shot down a 40° fan from a throwing circle that is 7 feet (2.135 m) in diameter and which features a wooden stopboard 4 inches (10 cm) high.

High jump

The high jump involves jumping over a horizontal bar, using body power and the momentum of a sprint. Unlike the long jump or the pole vault, the approach to the high jump is semi-circular in shape, allowing the athlete to make the approach from any angle. The style of the jump itself is up to the athlete, the only rule being that the takeoff for the jump is made from one foot. One technique above all else, however, has come to dominate—the "Fosbury Flop." This was developed by the U.S. athlete Dick Fosbury in the 1960s. It involves the athlete diving over the bar with a backward twist, landing on the crash mat with the shoulders and back. A rectangular crash-mat area 10 x 16 feet (3 x 5 m) provides a safe landing. Using the Fosbury Flop, athletes have achieved amazing heights—the Cuban athlete Javier Sotomayor jumped an incredible 8 feet (2.45 m) in 1993.

A shot putter drives his entire body weight behind a throw to achieve the best distance.

Long jump

The long jump is a distance-jumping competition. The athlete first makes a long sprint of around 131 feet (40 m). At a designated take-off board, the athlete leaps forward into a sand-filled landing about 9 feet (2.75 m) wide and 29 feet (9 m) long.

HEPTATHLON AND DECATHLON

Alongside individual field events, there are two mixed events. These test the athlete through a range of track and field challenges. The heptathlon is for women only and consists of seven events: 100 meters (110 yd) hurdles; high jump; shot put; 200 meters (220 yd) race; long jump; javelin; and 800 meters (875 yd) race. The decathlon is a male competition and has ten events: 100 meters sprint, long jump, shot put, high jump, 400 meters (440 yd) run, 100 meters hurdles, discus, javelin, pole vault, and 1,500 meters (1,640 yd) run. Both events are conducted over two days, with the middle-distance races being the final events.

Daley Thompson (U.K.) practices the long jump. His titles in the 1980s included four world records.

The distance jumped is measured from the take-off board to the first point of impact on the sand (the sand is raked flat after each competitor has jumped to show the impact point clearly). One of the greatest long jumpers of all time was the U.S. athlete Carl Lewis. He holds the men's indoor world record of 28 ft 10 in (8.79 m).

Pole vault

The pole vault is athletics' most spectacular event. The poles themselves are made of either fiberglass or carbon fiber (until around 1960, they were aluminum), and they are chosen by the athlete according to preference or the height of jump. To vault, the athlete runs along a 147-foot (45-m) track, then plants the tip of the pole in a **pole box** and uses the spring action of the pole to cross the bar. A height of 15 feet 6 inches (4.75 m) was achieved by the female Russian gymnast Svetlana Feofanova in 2002, while the athlete Sergei Bubka from the Ukraine (a country on the southwest border of the Russian Federation) cleared an incredible 20 feet 2 inches (6.15 m) in 1993.

Triple jump

The triple jump is essentially a long jump, but the athlete makes a hop and a step before the final jump. After running, the athlete launches from the take-off board with one leg, and lands on the same leg to make a hop. Then the other leg is used to make a step that launches her forward into the sand-filled landing area. As in long jump, the distance of the jump is measured from the take-off board to the first impression on the sand. Each stage of the triple jump covers about thirty-three percent of the total distance.

Brazil's Maurren Maggi makes the long jump. The heels are thrust well in front of the body to increase the distance from take-off point to landing.

Mental Preparation to Avoid Injury

The first ingredient of mental training for field events is commitment. Commitment to your sport means that your mind and body are 100 percent devoted to technical excellence and high achievement.

Many accidents occur among athletes who are mentally distracted while training or competing, or who do not have the discipline to train hard and master techniques. Commitment can help correct both of these problems.

COMMITMENT

If you find that your passion for the sport is weak, it may be that you are simply not interested enough in your sport. If this is the case, try something else. However, it may also be that you are not stimulated enough. Boredom kills commitment quickly, so invest in making your sport as interesting as possible:

- Find out almost everything you can about your sport, reading books, watching videos, and attending events.
- Talk with professional athletes. Many elite track and field competitors now have their own websites with e-mail links. Share your problems with them and you might find that they have also experienced the same problems.

An athlete has a moment of focus before his run up to the pole vault. Confidence is the key to an event such as pole vaulting, and confidence only comes from hard training and a supportive coach.

Eye focus is vital in javelin events. The athlete should concentrate his or her vision toward a defined point in the far distance and use all possible body strength to attempt to reach this point with the javelin.

- Make the effort to travel to watch world-class athletes compete, and be inspired by their performance.
- Organize social outings with other athletes and team members—training should be fun, not just hard work.
- Focus all your energies on winning a particular medal or competition.
- Keep a training journal that records everything about each training session and competition, as well as every bit of progress.

Try to think of as many ways as possible to feed both your imagination and your passion for your sport.

WORK AND DISCIPLINE

Passion is about dreams—dreaming about who you can become and what you can achieve. However, the hard fact is that, without work and discipline, the dreams will stay dreams and not become reality. The trick is to work out an action plan to take you step-by-step toward your goals. Do this through the following steps:

- Try to picture your ultimate goal, such as winning the world championships or a local title. Make this picture very clear. Be sure that it is what you really want.

- Working backward through time, think of every step you need to take to reach that final goal. For example, to win a regional title, you must first be selected for the team. To be selected, you must pass the team tryouts on a particular date. To pass the team tryouts, you must improve your qualifying performance in the long jump. To improve the qualifying performance—work backward in this way until you are at the present.

- What you now have is a breakdown of your major goal into small, manageable steps. Look at the first step on your list. Devote all your resources to achieving this goal. The important point is that for each step you develop an action plan. In short, an action plan is what you will actually do to make the step happen. Work out the practical needs and then, most importantly, start them now. Beware of phrases such as "I'll start this tomorrow." Once you have made the decision to achieve something, start working for it today.

Draw up an action plan for your training routine. At the beginning of each week, write down in a diary when you will train, what you will work on, and what you hope to achieve by the end of each session. Planning and preparation are what separates winners from other competitors. Keep a training log—a diary recording everything that happened during a particular training session or competition. The advantage of a well-kept training log is that you can see exactly what you need to work on. It can also reveal why you are suffering from certain injuries. You may notice, for example, that you have been suffering from shoulder pain only since you started attempting a new technique in shot put. This will indicate that you need to alter your technique or strengthen your shoulder muscles.

FEAR-CONTROL AND VISUALIZATION

By preparing fully and working hard on your technique, you will go a long way to mastering another problem—fear. Athletes can be afraid of many things: failure, injury, embarrassment, or letting the team down. Fear is a dangerous feeling to take into field events. Fear can take away your ability to concentrate and to move with confidence. In events such as the pole

A shot putter requires both coordination and strength to make power and technique work together.

vault, this can be lethal. When the vaulter is ascending heights of up to 52 feet 6 inches (16 m) on the pole, there is a point where she is upside down and facing away from the landing mat. All she can see is the hard ground beneath her. Any lapse in concentration at this point could result in a fatal fall. It is no coincidence that most serious sporting injuries happen at competitions: the pressure of the competition leads to an increase in fear and an equal increase in accidents.

The important point to realize is that fear is never entirely eradicated. What we need to do is control fear and use the energy it provides to help us perform better. Here are some of the best ways of getting fear to work for you:

- Counter any negative thoughts with positive thoughts. Instead of thinking "I really can't throw the discus any farther," think "I'm going to add an extra foot on to my distance." Counter every negative with a positive immediately.

- Take control of your body posture. Stand up straight, keep your chin up, look ahead, and make bold, confident movements with your entire body. Scientific research has shown that if you act confidently and assertively, even if you do not initially feel that way, your brain will eventually feel more assured.

- Control fear through knowledge. Remind yourself of how hard you have trained and how many times you have taken part in your event before. Focus your attention on the event, and this will draw attention away from your fear.

Visualization

Another method of handling fear, and also improving technique, is called **visualization**. Say you want to improve your hammer throw. Sitting quietly, close your eyes and picture yourself doing the throw perfectly. Open the power of your imagination. Imagine the sights and sounds of the training field as vividly as possible. Try to feel the movement of your arm muscles as you whip the hammer

Athletes have to train themselves to ignore the distractions surrounding them at competitions. The breathing must be controlled and the eyes focused only on the area of competition.

through the air. See the smooth lines of flight your body takes, and feel a sense of balance as you twist around. Finally, watch the hammer cutting through the air, sailing out into the fan. Pick out any pieces of technique you are struggling with, and concentrate on those in particular. If you are having trouble working out what the perfect technique may feel like, watch a video of a world-class competitor doing it. Then, in your mind's eye, project your own features onto those of the professional, and see yourself performing with excellence.

Scientific research shows that if the brain vividly imagines performing an action, the body learns that action as if it was actually training. Practice the action regularly and focus on visualizing the techniques which give you the most concern.

COACHING RELATIONSHIP

A good coach is as essential in track and field as in any other sport. There are literally thousands of track and field coaches in the United States. Picking out the professionals from the less qualified can be difficult, but remember, a good coach will:

- explain techniques clearly and simply;
- have approved coaching qualifications from a governing body such as USATF;
- make you feel good about yourself, and give you plenty of positive feedback;
- give you days off to rest your body and mind;
- have a clear structure and objective to every training session;

- understand the physiology and psychology of sports, and know how to handle injuries;
- Make time for extra training in preparation for competitions.

Track and field athlete, Jodi Anderson Hicks, receives some coaching in the shot put during the 1980s.

Physical Preparation

Preventing injury in sports requires increasing the strength and flexibility of vulnerable muscle groups and the muscles, tendons, and ligaments surrounding joints. The muscles and joints most at risk are those which endure repeated stress and heavy loads during exercise, or which are exposed to sudden explosive movements.

For example, triple jumpers are susceptible to overuse injuries in the muscles and **tendons** that join the thigh bone to the hip joint. By contrast, discus and javelin competitors are in danger of rupturing their back muscles from the twisting and hurling actions in their events.

DEMANDS ON THE BODY

Each field event places different demands on the human body. Athletes must, of course, have well-rounded physiques that are strong and flexible at every level. However, they must also condition the parts of the body that are put under the most stress by their chosen events. These are:

• Discus—shoulders, arms, lower back, hips, knees
• Javelin—shoulders, elbows, groin, upper and lower back, hips
• Hammer—shoulders, elbows, back, abdominals, hips, knees
• Shot put—shoulders, arms, abdominals, back, legs

Sprinting requires all-over body conditioning, not just strong legs. The arms and shoulders are used to "pump" the legs faster, while the torso muscles hold the body firm during the acceleration.

- High jump—spine, ankles, knees, hips
- Pole vault—shoulders, abdominals, back
- Long jump—ankles, knees, hips, back
- Triple jump—ankles, knees, hips, back

Athletes must give special attention to preparing the muscle groups and joints that are most worked by their sport.

STRENGTH TRAINING

Strength training basically means resistance exercises. Resistance exercises are those that use the muscles to lift, pull, or push weight. They result in stronger and larger muscles by producing more and tougher muscle fibers in order to cope with the increasing weight demands.

The best form of body-strengthening exercise is weight training. Weight training uses either **freeweights** or **weight machines** to strengthen the muscles. However, it carries substantial risks of injury if done incorrectly, especially among those under eighteen years of age. Always get professional training in using weights from your coach or other properly

Dumbbell flyes improve shoulders, biceps, and triceps. Breathe out when pushing the weights upward and in when relaxing them. Keep the feet flat on the floor.

qualified instructor; and, if you are under eighteen, follow these key rules for safe and effective results:

- When learning any new technique, practice it first without any weight at all until you can demonstrate perfect technique to an instructor. Once you have the right technique, add only light weights which you can handle easily.

- Add further weights in 1–3 pound (0.5–1.5 kg) increments, and perform 1–3 **sets** at the new weight. Once you can demonstrate perfect technique at the new weight, further weight can be added.

- Do not train more than three times a week, in thirty-minute sessions.

- Do all exercises slowly, with total control and concentration. It should take three full seconds to perform the **power phase** of the exercise, and three full seconds to relax the weight.

- Keep breathing deeply throughout the lift. Breathe out during the power phase, and in during the relaxation phase.

- Always warm up thoroughly before doing weights. Cold muscles are very much exposed to injury.

- Be systematic about how you develop your body. Always develop muscles in antagonistic pairs. This means

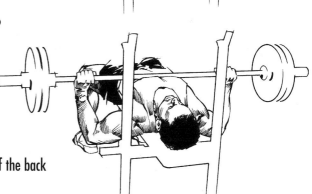

Always perform the bench press with a partner for safety, and use only light, comfortable weights. Keep the small of the back flat on the bench throughout.

that, if you develop the bicep on the inside of the arm, you develop the tricep on the outside of the arm equally. This concept also applies to the back and abdominals, and the **quadriceps** and **hamstrings**.

- Do not attempt heavy **deadlift** exercises. These put too much strain on the developing physique.

ENDURANCE

Endurance is a matter of **aerobic** training. An aerobic exercise is one which the body requires increased amounts of oxygen to perform. The body gets this oxygen by raising the heart and breathing rates, then sustaining both at the increased level. Aerobic exercise is vital for injury prevention because it strengthens the heart muscles and lungs to cope with strenuous exercise.

Fortunately, being a track-and-field athlete means that you probably get all the aerobic exercise you need from running. Do not, however, rely upon running alone. The best aerobic fitness comes from **cross training**, which entails mixing different aerobic events in your training schedule. Use two or three different types of aerobic training to ensure that your **cardiovascular** system is strong, and also to develop different muscle groups. An excellent combination would be running, swimming, and cycling: running and cycling improve lower limb flexibility and strength, while swimming enhances the shoulders, arms, back, and abdominals. One caution: even if you are very fit in one sport, begin your training in another by easing into it. Different sports have different muscular demands, so give your body time to acclimatize to the new exercise. Also, in all your training, make sure that you have at least two days a week of complete rest. Any less than that and you run a risk of injury through overtraining because your muscles will not have time to recover and strengthen.

Twenty to thirty minutes of running, three times a week, develops endurance useful for every field event, including throwing events.

FLEXIBILITY

Flexibility training is the systematic lengthening of muscles. A flexible muscle is far less likely to sustain injury under extreme stress because it has a greater range of movement before damage can occur.

Track and field events frequently require explosive stretching movements from the limbs during throwing, jumping, or sprinting. For this reason, track-and-field athletes should do at least twenty minutes of stretching exercises three times a week. Your coach will give you a full flexibility routine designed specifically for your sport. Every stretch must be practiced slowly and carefully. Never try to achieve dramatic levels of flexibility by pushing further than your body will allow. Stretching can easily result in ruptured muscles, tendons, and **ligaments**. It can take many months of diligent flexibility training to see significant improvement, so be patient.

Regardless of the type of stretch, obey these general rules:

- Stop immediately if you feel any sudden pains or growing burning sensations. Also stop if you feel nauseous, faint, or ill in any way.
- Keep breathing deeply throughout any stretch—your muscles need good supplies of oxygen to cope with the effort.

- Make sure that you stretch after you have completed your day's exercise. The muscles, tired and sore from overwork, recover more quickly if they are stretched as the body is cooling down. Stretching prevents the muscles from tightening up and becoming stiff.

PLYOMETRIC TRAINING

Plyometric training is relevant to any sport using sudden, explosive movements, so it is particularly important to field events. A relatively modern branch of sports training, it aims to condition the muscles to make contraction movements in the

Stretch the quadriceps by pulling the heel of each leg up toward the buttocks. Leaning forward as seen here will increase the intensity of the stretch, but only do this if you already have flexible limbs.

IMPORTANT STRETCHES

The following stretches are excellent for loosening up the hips, waist, and back—all areas that are prone to injury.

HIP/GROIN STRETCH

1. Stand with your legs in a "A"-shape about two shoulder-widths apart.
2. Bend forward from the waist, and take your body weight on your hands.
3. Slowly sink your hips downward, inching your legs wider and wider apart. Keep breathing deeply.
4. When you are at your limit, hold the position for five to ten seconds and try to relax. You may then be able to go down farther.
5. When you have reached your maximum stretch, come out of it by walking your feet inward (while maintaining your weight on your hands) until you are able to stand up.

WAIST AND BACK STRETCH

1. Stand upright, with your feet a shoulder-width apart.
2. Bend straight forward from the waist, and lower your torso as far as it will go, keeping your back straight.
3. Hold the legs and gently pull on them to go down farther. Hold the stretch for ten seconds, then move your body upright again.
4. Put your hands against your lower back and stretch your body backward, looking up at the ceiling as you do. Do not bend your head too far, as this could lead to a neck strain. Hold for ten seconds.

shortest possible periods of time. Plyometrics need to be specifically tailored to the individual sport. Therefore, if you are a discus or javelin thrower, focus on upper-body plyometrics. If you do the long jump, lower-body plyometrics are required.

Specific plyometric exercises concentrate on short, vigorous movements followed instantly by a relaxation phase. They are now an essential part of any field athlete's training regime because they are useful for reducing incidences of ruptures from sudden movements, but make sure that you learn them under a qualified tutor. There are numerous plyometric exercises. Again, your coach should be able to provide you with a routine specific to your event. Here are two plyometric exercises, however, to demonstrate the technique:

Upper body

The athlete lies on the floor with a partner standing over him. The partner drops a medicine ball from a height at the chest of the athlete. The athlete catches the ball and immediately throws it back. This exercise trains the rapid expansion and contraction of the arms and is useful for throwing events.

Lower body

The athlete jumps from the ground onto a box or step between 12 and 31 inches (30–80 cm) high, then immediately jumps back off. This exercise should be practiced carefully, beginning with the lower height and working upward. It conditions the legs for sprint starts and for jumping events.

WARMING UP

Warming up means raising the temperature of the muscles ready for exercise. It is one of the most important stages of a training session. Cold muscles are stiff and inflexible, and more easily injured. Also, if you go straight into vigorous exercise without warming up, your heart and lungs may struggle to cope with the sudden effort, leading to nausea and dizziness.

A warm-up need take no longer than ten minutes. The first five minutes involves gentle exercise to raise the heart and breathing rates slightly and to make the body feel warmer. To do this, try light jogging on the spot, **star jumps**, or a vigorous walk around the athletic track. Whatever you do, do not push the exercise hard, and keep the body loose and relaxed. After five minutes, stop and shake the limbs to get rid of any remaining tension. Then you need to stretch.

Warm-up stretching is focused on the major muscle groups of the body. Working from the ankles to the neck (or vice versa), do a simple stretch for each large muscle group. Take care not to overstretch because the muscles may still be a little stiff despite the preceding exercise. Focus especially on those areas of the body which will be used most in the event.

Good preparation for training and competing means less likelihood of injury. Such preparation needs discipline, but it is worth the investment for your own safety.

This stretch improves groin, hip, and hamstring flexibility. Move slowly, breathing deeply throughout the stretch.

Using Equipment Safely

Field events can be extremely hazardous. While long jump and triple jump are relatively safe, events such as the pole vault and hammer throw are potentially lethal. To prevent accidents, it is imperative that you use the equipment safely.

Jumping events involve more accidents than any other element of track and field, particularly at school level. Excluding for the moment the pole vault, which is a special case, some of the biggest dangers surround the high jump.

High-jump accidents tend to be the result of falls and the incorrect use of the high-jump equipment. The best protection in the case of a fall are the safety mats:

- Before attempting a jump, examine the crash mats to make sure that there are no gaps between mats.
- Look to see that the mats have not shifted after each jump.
- If the jump is inside, check that the apparatus and mats are set up well away from walls. Too close, and the athlete runs the risk of bouncing off the mats into a wall.
- Confirm that the mats are of the correct type.

High-jump athletes are exposed to injury when the equipment is set up by inexperienced individuals. The marker supports should not be facing toward you. If they are, this means that the marker will not fall off if you strike it. Instead, the

Javelin events are most dangerous for those downfield of the throw. When practicing, organize a routine so that everyone throws and everyone collects together at the signal of the instructor.

Kelly Sotherton of the United Kingdom crosses the high jump in the heptathlon. High-jump equipment should feature very stable standards and a crossbar which is dislodged with the lightest of touches.

standards (the pieces at the side supporting the crossbar) will come crashing down on top of you as you hit the mats. An even worse mistake is to replace lost markers with pieces of twine or string. This is unacceptable: not only can the twine cause a cut if you strike it, but the standards can also be pulled down on top of you.

THROWING EVENTS

The discus, hammer, shot put, and javelin are risky for the obvious reason that heavy or pointed objects are being thrown at high speeds. The throwing area must be entirely clear of people before participants start training or competing, and crowds should be kept back in demarcated areas—never let them gather along the sector lines.

Never throw anything until your coach or a competition official gives you permission to do so, and never practice swinging or throwing the implement outside the safety cage. Have a proper procedure for retrieving the implements you have thrown: nobody else should enter the cage when you are out in the throwing area.

Part of your training should include recovering an out-of-control technique within the cage. Loss of control happens mainly in the discus, hammer throw, and shot put, when the athlete loses balance during the spinning build-up to the throw. When this happens, try not to release the implement—it will be a danger both to yourself and others—unless holding onto it will present a greater risk. Wind the spin down slowly, keeping the object under control until it stops.

Check out the quality of equipment before you train or compete. Discuses should be free of chips, cracked rubber, or splits. Hammer wires must be free from any fraying and firmly attached to the handles. Javelin points should be securely fixed to the shaft. Look downward and check the quality of the throwing circle beneath your feet. Have it swept of any dirt or debris, and make sure that any damage to its surface is repaired. Finally, examine the protective cage around the throwing circle. Most importantly, it should have no holes in its structure, and it must be securely fastened down. A shot put can weigh over 15 pounds (7 kg) and travel at 31 miles per hour (50 km/h) from the hands of an expert, so the cord or metal wire of the cage must be in pristine condition to withstand a blow.

POLE VAULT

The pole vault is one of the most dangerous events in sports, not just in track and field. The vaulting area must be extremely well protected with crash mats on the landing area and to the side of the vault box, all of which must be fixed securely in place. No concrete areas should be exposed, and any hard surfaces must be

Make sure that the shot put is securely located between hand, shoulder, and chin before winding up to throw. A poor grip can result in the shot slipping out before the throw and causing injury.

covered with at least 2 inches (5 cm) of foam padding. Remove any litter or implements from the landing area, and also check the approach and pole box for any obstructions. The pole box must have its frontal lip below ground level and ideally should be a different color from the approach track to make it stand out.

The pole itself needs to be properly chosen for your level of ability and also your body weight. Choosing the incorrect pole is extremely serious and could lead to a fall from a broken pole. Check the pole over thoroughly. Do not use it if you can see cracks or deep scratches. Make the pole safer to use by putting grip tape around the shaft. Grip tape gives the hands a better grip on the pole, and prevents slipping.

Vaulting is an advanced skill, so attempt it only if you have all the necessary training and experience. Warm up completely beforehand, and focus your mind on what is ahead. Focus all your attention on landing in the pit with the proper technique—your hips and back should take the landing, never your feet. A recommended additional piece of safety equipment is a good athletic crash helmet. These are made from high-impact plastics and are extremely light. Should you fall onto hard ground, they can protect you from serious head injury.

PERSONAL EQUIPMENT

Your personal equipment and clothing have a bearing both on how you compete and how safely you compete. Here are some tips for what you should and should not pack and wear:

- Do not wear any jewelry at all while competing in field events.
- Your footwear must be purposely designed for the event and must fit properly. Purchase footwear only from reputable athletics suppliers, and wear it only for training or competing, never for daily use.
- Magnesium powder is useful for drying out sweating hands for the pole vault.
- Pack high energy foods for a day's training or competing. These include fruit juice, pasta, salads, low-sugar cereal bars, and fruit (especially bananas).
- Pack warm fleece-lined training jackets and trousers to go over your shorts and T-shirt when you are not training or competing. These will help your muscles stay warm after the warm-up.

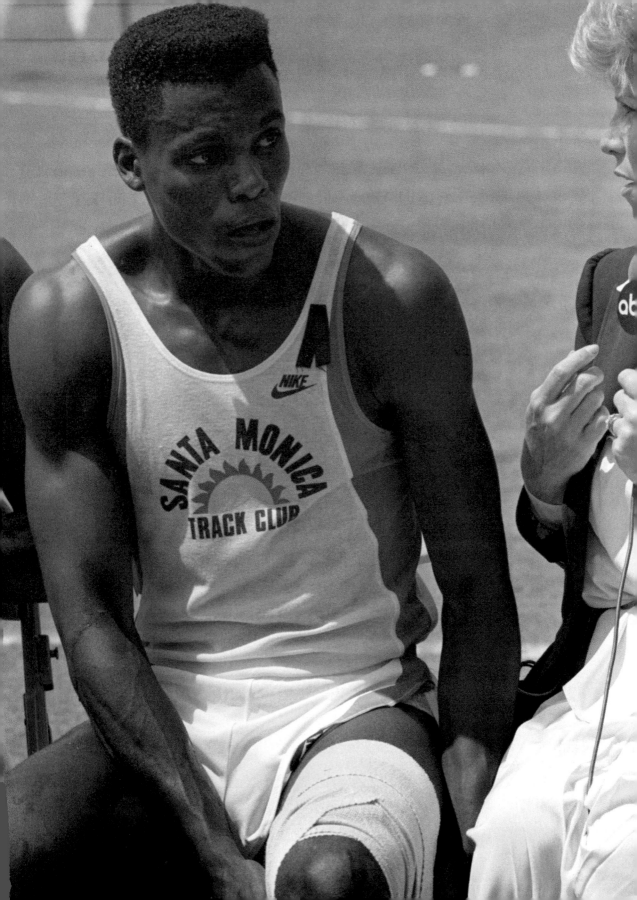

Treating Common Injuries

Sports injuries usually happen suddenly through an accident or strain, or gradually through wear and tear over a period of time. Both types of injury can stop an athletic career if not handled properly.

The reason for athletic injuries has changed over the past forty years. In the 1960s, most injuries in athletics were the result of accidents. Today, the majority of injuries result from overuse.

"Overuse" simply means that the muscles and joints of the body are worked harder than they are meant to be. If you train every day of the week for several hours, and rarely take a rest, then your muscles and joints do not have proper recovery time to stay healthy. Overtraining is a classic problem in preparation for competitions. Athletes push themselves harder and harder, but end up performing poorly on the day because they are physically exhausted, and often injure themselves through overuse.

The best treatment for overuse injuries is prevention rather than cure. Have a sensible training regime. Allow at least two days each week for complete rest to give your body time to recuperate. Warm up properly before every training session or competition, using gentle exercise and stretching. Make sure that all

Track and field star Carl Lewis sits on a bench with a bandage wrapped around his injured hamstring at the USA Track and Field Championship in 1987.

SYMPTOMS OF OVERUSE INJURIES

Overuse injuries present with both mental and physical symptoms.

1. MENTAL SYMPTOMS:

- unusual tiredness or fatigue;
- feeling very emotional, particularly depressed, anxious, or stressed;
- feelings of guilt about any time you are not training;
- a lack of appetite;
- an inability to sleep at night.

2. PHYSICAL SYMPTOMS:

- muscle soreness and cramps;
- stiff, painful, or unstable joints;
- problems getting certain parts of the body comfortable in bed at night;
- tension headaches;
- painful tendons;
- pain that shows no improvement after three days.

Despite suffering a serious spinal injury during a training session, Emma George has maintained her status as one of the world's best pole vaulters.

footwear and personal equipment is properly fitted or designed for your body. If you sense an injury developing, decrease your training activity. If possible, concentrate on other events or techniques to give the injury a rest—but this can be very difficult in field events, which often use every muscle in the body.

If the injury does not heal itself through reduced training, go to a doctor, especially if the pain lasts more than three days. However, if the injury is a simple strained muscle or aching joint, try the **P.R.I.C.E.** method of self-treatment (see page 44).

RANGE OF MOTION EXERCISES

P.R.I.C.E. may resolve the problem by itself. Two further stages of treatment may be required if the injury has been more severe, such as a badly twisted ankle or a sprained shoulder. When the pain has subsided, use range of motion (**R.O.M.**) exercises. These are light stretching and flexibility exercises designed to give the joint or limb its full range of movement. Using gentle stretches, work a limb or joint through the full range of its normal flexibility. The body will be sensitive to reinjury, so work up your flexibility gradually. Do not use bouncing or jerking actions to push the stretch farther.

Once you have full, pain-free R.O.M., you must strengthen the injured joint or muscle for the return to training. Do this using resistance exercises with light weights—no more than 1–3 pounds (0.5–1.5 kg) at first. Alternatively, do simple bodyweight strengthening exercises, such as lunges and angled push-ups—light push-ups against the edge of a table also work well. Do all exercises gently with no strenuous or rapid movements. Build up the weight or resistance gradually over a period of several days (or even weeks if the injury was severe) until you are back to normal levels. Stop training or reduce the weights used if the pain returns or you experience any burning sensations in the joint or muscle.

PROTECTION, REST, ICE, COMPRESSION, ELEVATION (P.R.I.C.E.)

PROTECTION: Stop training immediately and protect the injured area from further damage by restricting all unnecessary activity.

REST: Give the injured area complete rest for at least a week. Restrict other activities and sports that affect the injury.

ICE: Reduce any swelling around the injury by applying ice packs two or three times a day, for no longer than twenty minutes each time. If there is no swelling, however, try heat treatments. Heat-generating ointments (available from drug stores) are good for reducing pain in muscle strains. Do not use heat treatments on swelling areas.

COMPRESSION: Wrap the injury firmly with an elastic bandage, sports tape, or a professional compression bandage to reduce swelling and protect the joint or muscle against further damage.

ELEVATION: Elevate an injured limb. If the leg is injured, try to raise it higher than the hips; if the arm is injured, try to position your hand higher than the shoulder. Elevation reduces the amount of blood flowing into a limb, and this helps reduce swelling.

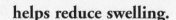
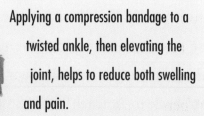

Applying a compression bandage to a twisted ankle, then elevating the joint, helps to reduce both swelling and pain.

Now we will look at the injuries specific to each type of field event and consider what can be done about them.

THROWING INJURIES

Throwing injuries mainly affect the upper limbs. Discus throwing, shot put, javelin, and hammer throw all have different actions, but all put immense strain upon the shoulder's **rotator cuff**, the **biceps** and **triceps** in the arms, and the elbow. The elbow and shoulder suffer the most injuries.

The rotator cuff in the shoulder is the group of muscles and tendons that attach the upper-arm bone (the humerus) to the shoulder joint and also enable the arm's rotational movement. The rotator cuff accounts for more than seventy-five percent of all shoulder injuries in sports. During throwing events, it has to cope with the cocking of the arm ready to throw, the sudden acceleration of the arm as the object is thrown, and the equally sudden stopping of the arm at the end of the throw. When these actions are repeated over and over again, muscles in the rotator cuff can be torn or ruptured.

SHOULDER MUSCLES

The shoulder is powered by a complex arrangement of muscles surrounding the joint.

Deltoid muscle — enables the arm to rotate, flex, and lift

Subscapularis muscle (part of the rotator cuff) — keeps the shoulder stable and rotates the humerus bone

Biceps muscle — aids movement of the arm and shoulder joint

Athletes throwing shot puts and hammers are particularly prone to rotator cuff injuries because of the weight of the object being thrown.

Symptoms of a damaged rotator cuff include:

- intense pain in the shoulder, which may radiate down the upper arm;
- an increase in pain when the arm is rotated or when attempting to lift objects;
- a concentration of pain at night in bed, and the inability to make yourself comfortable because of the shoulder pain;
- limited movement of the arm;
- an inflamed shoulder joint;
- weakness in the movement of the arm at some points;
- clicking and popping sensations in the shoulder during movement.

Rotator cuff injuries

Rehabilitating a torn rotator cuff begins with total rest from training. Reduce arm activity to a minimum until the pain in the shoulder has subsided, which may take about a week. Use the P.R.I.C.E. procedure and also, under the guidance of a doctor or pharmacist, use painkillers and **anti-inflammatories** to bring pain and swelling under control.

R.O.M. exercises can be as simple as moving the arm gently through its full range of movement. To strengthen the shoulder, try upper-arm weight-training exercises

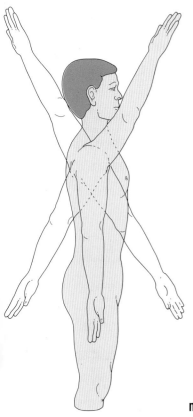

Gentle rotational movements forward and backward can bring back full range of movement to an injured shoulder joint.

using light 1-pound (500-g) dumbbells. Vary the exercises frequently to strengthen all parts of the rotator cuff. The following are two typical exercises:

- Hold the dumbbell to the side of the body, then raise your arm straight out to the side until it is at shoulder height. The thumb should be pointing downward. Hold for three seconds, then gently lower. Repeat two more times.
- Hold the dumbbell to the side of the body, then swing it forward with a straight arm until your arm reaches a vertical position with the dumbbell above your head. Hold for three seconds, then gently lower. Repeat.

Elbow injuries

Elbow injuries are common in all throwing events, but especially in the javelin and discus. When a thrower winds up for the throw, the throwing arm trails behind with the elbow locked under high G-forces. Then the elbow is whipped straight during the throw, particularly if the thrower's technique is poor. The classic injury to the elbow from field events is aptly called "thrower's elbow." Symptoms of this are:

- pain concentrated on the inside of the elbow, often radiating out into the arm;
- pain intensifying when the hand is turned palm downward to apply pressure;
- weakness in the wrist;
- the elbow joint being tender to the touch.

Thrower's elbow, and many other non-severe elbow injuries, can be treated with P.R.I.C.E., R.O.M., and strengthening exercises. Start the R.O.M. exercises as soon as possible. The elbow has a tendency to stiffen up dramatically after injury, and can degenerate further if the joint is not loosened. Elbow R.O.M. exercises are simple and can be done anywhere. Try this easy exercise:

1. Stand up straight with the arm by your side, palm facing up.
2. Slowly bend your elbow as far as possible, drawing your hand up to your

shoulder. Hold for three seconds, then lower slowly.

3. Repeat ten times.

To strengthen the elbow, perform the same exercise using a light dumbbell.

JUMPING INJURIES

The main body parts affected by jumping events are the ankle, knee, hamstrings, and spine. Ankles and knees suffer mainly from sudden thrusting forces as the jumper begins the sprint, then pushes off violently for the jump itself. In the case of long jumpers and triple jumpers, the lower limbs also have to withstand impact in the sand pit.

Ankle and knee joints can develop a range of problems from jumping activities, including in particular torn

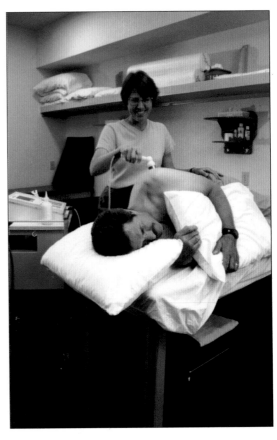

Ultrasound massage stimulates the muscles with penetrating sound waves that are inaudible to the ear. It is a common procedure in physical therapy.

muscles, tendons, and ligaments. The symptoms of these injuries include reduced mobility, pain, difficulty in putting pressure on the joint, limping, and general discomfort. P.R.I.C.E. will control the swelling and pain of the injury. Like the elbow, the ankle and knee joints benefit from early R.O.M., but keep these light to prevent overworking the already damaged joint.

- For the knee, try sitting on a high chair or table, moving the lower leg backward and forward through its full range of movement to reintroduce mobility. This will also serve to strengthen the knee joint.

- For the ankle, simply circle the foot in both directions and pull gently backward and forward to release its movement.

- An additional ankle-strengthening exercise is to slowly raise yourself up on tiptoe and hold for five seconds, then lower yourself back down.

Strengthening the knee and ankle can be done by walking:

- Walk on flat surfaces only, slowly building up to inclines for increased strengthening. Be particularly careful when walking down hills and steps. Many knee and ankle injuries are made worse by downward movement, so test your legs first on a short incline before attempting an entire hillside.

As with all the injuries described, stop rehabilitation exercises immediately if you have any sudden or growing pains.

ANKLE/CALF INJURIES

The diagram indicates muscles commonly injured in the lower leg and ankle.

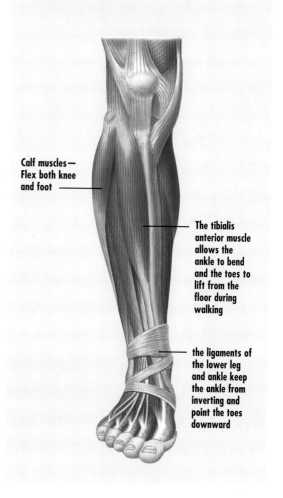

Calf muscles—
Flex both knee
and foot

The tibialis anterior muscle allows the ankle to bend and the toes to lift from the floor during walking

the ligaments of the lower leg and ankle keep the ankle from inverting and point the toes downward

Hamstring injuries

The hamstrings are commonly damaged in jumping events. They are a group of three muscles set at the back of each thigh which flex the knee joint. They are usually damaged in sprinting, especially during explosive starts from the blocks and fast accelerations. The injured person may feel a distinctive popping sensation at the moment of rupture, followed by pain at the back of the thigh and limited mobility in the knee. Sometimes there may be swelling and even bruising behind the knee.

Most hamstring injuries are fully treatable by following the P.R.I.C.E., R.O.M., and strengthening procedures. For the R.O.M. stage, use the following exercise:

• Sit on the edge of a table, with one leg over the edge of the table and the other running straight along the side. Keeping the back straight, bend forward from the waist over the outstretched leg until you feel a stretch in the back of the thigh and hamstrings. Hold for fifteen to twenty seconds, then release. Repeat the sequence five times. Repeat the exercises for the other leg.

BACK INJURIES

Both jumping and throwing competitors are exposed to back injuries. The back undergoes extreme twisting forces during field events. Muscles are easily ruptured, and even the spine itself can be damaged. Back injuries should always be seen by a doctor because some can be very serious.

The most common injury is pulled back muscles. Its main symptom is severe pain in the lower back, made worse through movement or lifting. Treat initially with complete rest, lying down as much as possible on a firm supporting surface. Drawing your knees up with the feet flat on the surface will ease the pain by pushing the small of the back down on to the bed for support.

As the pain diminishes, introduce light exercise to increase flexibility and strength:

• For the standing side bend, stand straight up with your feet shoulder-width apart. Gently run your left hand down the side of your left thigh, stretching the torso over to the side. Repeat on the right-hand side. Repeat set three times.

Massage by a qualified physical therapist can alleviate stiffness in muscles and help the return of flexibility to a damaged muscle. It can even be part of a warm-up.

• Next, place your hands on either side of your spine in the small of your back. Lean the upper body gently backward while looking upward at the ceiling.

Then perform light warm-up routines involving crunches and the lightest of weight-training exercises with small weight loads. Work on sitting and standing with correct posture. The back should be straight with the shoulders drawn backward—imagine that you are being drawn up straight via a rope attached to the top of your head. Take hot baths to apply heat treatment to the injured muscles.

Careers in Field Athletics

Making a career in any sort of sport requires the utmost self-discipline. You must design a plan of action to get to where you want to be, then a rigorous training program to turn that plan into reality.

Your ability to advance in the world of track and field depends upon three elements: times, heights, and distance. The system of advancement in U.S. track and field is very democratic. You will be able to move up the competition ladder as long as you make the qualifying grades in your running, throwing, and jumping. In short, the ability to progress rests upon your shoulders.

You have to be realistic about making it to the very top. Hundreds of thousands of young people participate in athletics each year. Top events for young people— such as the USATF National Junior Olympic Track and Field Championships— attract around 6,000 competitors, a small percentage of those who pursue track and field. Of those competitors, an even smaller number will go on to compete at higher levels, usually only those who place in the first three in each event.

If you are truly determined to be the best, plan your training meticulously. Work out which events are your strongest, then find out the times you need for entering the major competitions open to your age group. Discuss your intentions with your

Jonathan Edwards (United Kingdom) started triple-jumping in school. After entering professional athletics in the late 1980s, he set a new world record in the triple jump in 1995 and won numerous titles.

coach, then let the hard work begin. Expect to be training at least four or five days a week, for two or three hours each day. Do not, however, overtrain. Training to excess will generally spoil your performance rather than improve it.

TARGETS

Do not expect to head for Junior Olympics competitions immediately. Attend local and regional competition events, which offer you a realistic chance of doing well and enable you to gain invaluable competition experience. Only when you are physically or mentally prepared should you step up to the next level.

Track and field athletics in the United States are governed by the organization USA Track and Field (USATF). More than 4,000 USATF events are held each year, ranging from local interschool competitions to national and international

competitions. The USATF "Junior" and "Youth" programs give young athletes their first major chance to compete at national standards. The Youth events are open to any athlete who is a USATF member and belongs to one of five different age groups: Bantam, for ages 10 and under; Midget, for ages 11–12; Youth, for ages 13–14; Intermediate, for ages 15–16; and Young Men/Women, for ages 17–18. Though it is open to all, the USA Youth Outdoor Track and Field Championships are suitable for advanced athletes only.

The USATF issues performance guidelines showing what sort of times, distances, and heights you must meet if you are to compete on a level with the rest.

A long view of an athletic stadium. More than twenty individual events are held in such a stadium, the field events concentrated in the central portion surrounded by the six- or eight-lane running track.

MAKING THE GRADE

The following are samples of the qualifying standards needed for the U.S. Olympic Track and Field Trials:

Event	Men	Women
High jump	7 ft 5$^3/_4$ in (2.28 m)	6 ft 2 in (1.88 m)
Long jump	26 ft 6 in (8.1 m)	21 ft 4 in (6.5 m)
Shot put	65 ft 7 in (20 m)	57 ft 5 in (17.5 m)
Discus	208 ft 3$^1/_2$ in (63.5 m)	196 ft 10 in (60 m)
Hammer	229 ft 7 in (70 m)	218 ft (66.5 m)

The USATF Junior Championship events differ from the Youth events because qualifying times, distances, and heights must be met in order to qualify. These will be recorded at other USATF events or college or high school meets, and submitted to USATF prior to the competition. In addition to the qualifying standards, you must also be between fourteen and twenty years old to compete. Athletes who are 1 inch (3 cm) below the standards for discus, javelin, or hammer, or $^3/_8$ inch (1 cm) below the standards in the other events can compete if there are not enough qualified competitors.

At the top of the young person's track and field calendar is the National Junior Olympic Championships. This consists of a series of meets working up to a final championship. The meets are at Preliminary, Association, Regional, and National level. Each level requires qualifying standards, and the athlete has to work through each level in turn. Making it to the final championships is an exciting honor.

Winning a title opens up the possibility of competing in international **IAAF** Junior Olympic competitions and traveling around the world. Many J.O.C. finalists have also gone on to become members of the U.S. National Team as adults.

CAREER ATHLETES

For top national athletes over eighteen years old, there is the possibility of making the U.S. National Track and Field team. As with the young persons' competitions, trials and competitions for the adult national team require qualifying standards to be met for entry. Those who can meet such standards are few and far between. U.S.A. National Team athletes often hold world records in their chosen event. They have the opportunity to travel the world, competing in events such as the IAAF World Indoor Track and Field Championships, as well as the Olympics themselves.

Reaching the summit of athletic achievement demands a huge degree of commitment and natural talent. You must have an excellent coach, who systematically develops your performance, but also keeps an eye on your emotional welfare

Randy Barnes (U.S.A.) is one of the world's best shot putters, winning his first Olympic gold in Seoul, South Korea, in 1988.

MELISSA MUELLER

Since 1997, Mel Mueller has been one of the foremost female pole vaulters in the United States. At school, she trained mainly in heptathlon until her fifth year, when the college coach encouraged her to try the vault. Her credits include 2nd place at the 1999 and 2000 U.S.A. Indoor championships, 5th at the 1999 World Championships, and 3rd at the 2000 Olympic trials. She has also had to battle with injury. In 2001, she underwent knee surgery. Despite a long period of recuperation, Mel returned to competition later in the year and has vaulted 15 feet (4.6 m) and higher in both the 2001 outdoor and 2002 indoor competitions.

as well. You must gain as much experience as possible on the competition circuit, and add medals to your wall to increase your confidence. If you attend a university after high school, you can help your track and field progress by picking one that has a top-level university athletics squad. There are many to choose from across the United States, including Louisiana State University, University of Pennsylvania, University of Texas, and the University of California at Los Angeles. Doing track and field at a university can lead to national level status if you are committed, but remember to concentrate equally on your academic studies—an athletics career is relatively short, but your academic qualifications will last you a lifetime.

Jackie Joyner-Kersee of the United States makes a spectacular jump in the IAAF World Championships in Athens, 1997. Despite battling against severe asthma, she became a World and Olympic record holder.

Glossary

Aerobic: Exercise that demands increased oxygen and so forces up the heart and breathing rates.

Anti-inflammatories: Any medication that reduces swelling.

Biceps: The large muscles on the inside of the upper arm, which flex the arm and forearm.

Cardiovascular: "Cardiovascular exercise" is any exercise that improves the health and function of the heart and lungs.

Cross training: Mixing various sports in a training program to improve fitness.

Deadlift: A lift from a standing position without using any support equipment such as a bench.

Freeweights: Weight-training equipment consisting simply of a bar onto which weights are placed.

Hamstrings: The group of three muscles set at the back of the thigh.

IAAF: International Association of Athletics Federations, a major governing body for international athletics.

Ligament: A short band of tough body tissue, which connects bones or holds together joints.

Plyometric: Describing exercises that are designed to speed up explosive and sudden muscular movements.

Pole box: The slot in the ground in which a pole vaulter lodges the tip of the pole for launch.

Power phase: In weight training, the phase where the weight is lifted, pulled, or pushed.

P.R.I.C.E.: An acronym for the common method for treating non-serious sprains and strains—Protection, Rest, Ice, Compression, Elevation.

Quadriceps: The large four-part muscle on the front of each thigh, used to extend the leg.

R.O.M.: Abbreviation for Range of Motion, which refers to exercises designed to reintroduce flexibility into an injured joint or muscle.

Rotator cuff: The group of muscles holding the shoulder joint in place, enabling the rotational movement of the arm.

Set: A complete group of repetitions.

Star jumps: An exercise in which the athlete jumps in and out of an "X" shape made with his arms and legs.

Stopboard: A raised feature at the edge of a discus, hammer-throw, or shot-put circle, beyond which the athlete must not step when making a throw.

Tendon: A cord of body tissue connecting a muscle to a bone.

Triceps: The muscles on the back of the upper arm.

Visualization: A technique for improving sports performance by training in the imagination.

Weight machines: Machines providing various resistance exercises used in weight training.

Further Information

USEFUL WEB SITES

For news and events on track and field in the U.S., try:

www.american-trackandfield.com

International Association of Athletics Federations: www.iaaf.org

For general articles and news on track and field throughout the world:

www.track-and-field.net

U.S.A. Track and Field: www.usatf.org

The Web sites listed on this page were active at the time of publication. The publisher is not responsible for Web sites that have changed their address or discontinued operation since the date of publication. The publisher will review and update the Web sites upon each reprint.

FURTHER READING

Alter, Michael J. *Sport Stretch—311 Stretches for 41 Sports*. Champaign, Illinois: Human Kinetics, 1998.

Carr, Gerland. *Fundamentals of Track and Field*. Champaign, Illinois: Human Kinetics, 2000.

Faigenbaum, Avery and Wayne Westcott. *Strength and Power Training for Young Athletes*. Champaign, Illinois: Human Kinetics, 2000.

Guthrie, Mark. *Coaching Track and Field Successfully*. Champaign, Illinois: Human Kinetics, 2003.

Rodgers, Joseph L. *U.S.A. Track and Field Coaching Manual*. Champaign, Illinois: Human Kinetics, 1999.

THE AUTHOR

Dr. Chris McNab is a writer and editor specializing in sports, survival, and other human-performance topics. He has written more than twenty-five books, and recent publications include *Survival First Aid*, *Martial Arts for People with Disabilities*, *Living Off the Land*, and *How to Pass the SAS Selection Course*. Chris lives in South Wales, U.K.

THE CONSULTANTS

Susan Saliba, Ph.D., is a senior associate athletic trainer and a clinical instructor at the University of Virginia in Charlottesville, Virginia. A certified athletic trainer and licensed physical therapist, Dr. Saliba provides sports medicine care, including prevention, treatment, and rehabilitation for the varsity athletes at the University. Dr. Saliba holds dual appointments as an Assistant Professor in the Curry School of Education and the Department of Orthopaedic Surgery. She is a member of the National Athletic Trainers' Association's Educational Executive Committee and its Clinical Education Committee.

Eric Small, M.D., a Harvard-trained sports medicine physician, is a nationally recognized expert in the field of sports injuries, nutritional supplements, and weight management programs. He is author of *Kids & Sports* (2002) and is Assistant Clinical Professor of Pediatrics, Orthopedics, and Rehabilitation Medicine at Mount Sinai School of Medicine in New York. He is also Director of the Sports Medicine Center for Young Athletes at Blythedale Children's Hospital in Valhalla, New York. Dr. Small has served on the American Academy of Pediatrics Committee on Sports Medicine for the past six years, where he develops national policy regarding children's medical issues and sport

Index

Page numbers in *italics* refer to
photographs and illustrations.

accidents 35–9, 41 *see also* injuries
action plans, training 19–20, 23, 25–6,
　27–8, 53–4
aerobic training 28
ankle injuries 48–9

back injuries *42*, 50–1
Barnes, Randy *57*
bench presses *27*

career development 53–9
coaches 23, 32, 54, 57–8
commitment 17–18, 53–4, 57
competitions 53–7, 58
compression bandages *41*, 44
crash helmets 39
crash mats 13, 35, 37–8
cross training 28

decathlon 14
discus *8*, 9, 10, 11–12

Edwards, Jonathan *52*
elbow injuries 47–8
endurance training 28
equipment 11–13, 15, 35–9, 43
exercises, range of motion 43, 46–9, 50–1

fear, controlling 20–1
field events
　demands on the body 25–6
　origins 9–10
　see also individual events
flexibility 29–30, 31, 50–1
footwear 39, 43
Fosbury, Dick 13

goals, achieving 19–20

hammer throw 10, *11*, 12, 21–2
hamstring injuries 49–50
heptathlon 14, *36*
high jump 9, 13, 35–6

IAAF (International Association of
Athletics Federations) 57

injuries
　back *42*, 50–1
　jumping 48–50
　overuse 25, 41–3
　P.R.I.C.E treatment 43, 44, 46, 47,
　　48, 50
　stretching 29–30, 50–1
　throwing 45–8
　weight training 26–7, 46–7, 51

javelin 9, *10*, 11, *18, 34*
Joyner-Kersee, Jackie *59*

knee injuries 48–50, 58

Lewis, Carl 7, *40*
long jump 9, 13–14, *15, 59*

massage 48, *51*
mental preparation 17–23
Mueller, Mel 58
muscles
　back 50–1
　developing 26–8
　flexibility 29–30, 31, 32–3
　rotator cuff 45–7

Olympic Games 10, 56, 57
overtraining 41, 54
overuse injuries 25, 41–3

pain 42, 43–4, 46, 47, 48, 50
physical preparation 25–33
plyometric training 30, 32
pole vault 10, 15, *16, 22*, 37–9, *42*, 58
positive thinking 21, 23
preparation
　mental 17–23
　physical 25–33
　see also training
Protection, Rest, Ice, Compression, and
　Elevation (P.R.I.C.E.) 43, 44, 46, 47,
　48, 50

qualifying standards 53, 55–6

range of motion (R.O.M.) exercises 43,
　46–9, 50–1
rest periods 23, 28, 41, 44, 46

safety, equipment 35–9
shot put 9, 12, *13, 20*, 37, *38, 57*
shoulder injuries 45–7
strength training 26–8
stretching 29–30, 31, 33, 50–1

Thompson, Daley *14*
training
　action plans 19–20, 23, 25–6, 27–8,
　　53–4
　endurance 28
　flexibility 29–30, 31, 50–1
　plyometric 30, 32
　record-keeping 18, 19–20
　strength 26–8
　weights 26–8, 46–7, 51
triple jump 15, *52*

ultrasound massage *48*,
universities 58
USA Track and Field (USATF) 53–6

visualization 21–2

warming up 27, 32–3, 41, 51
weight training 26–8, 46–7, 51